Webster's New World

Guide To

Punctuation

Webster's New World

Guide To

Punctuation

Auriel Douglas

Michael Strumpf

Prentice Hall

New York • London • Toronto • Sydney • Tokyo • Singapore

WEBSTER'S NEW WORLD

Simon & Schuster, Inc.
15 Columbus Circle
New York, NY 10023

DISTRIBUTED BY PRENTICE HALL TRADE SALES

Manufactured in the United States of America

    5 6 7 8 9 10

Library of Congress Cataloging-in-Publication Data

Strumpf, Michael.
  Webster's New World guide to punctuation /
Michael Strumpf and Auriel Douglas.
    p. cm.
  Includes index.
  ISBN 0-13-947896-5
  1. English language—Punctuation. I. Douglas,
Auriel.
II. Title.
PE1450.S76 1988   88-7290
428.2—dc19   CIP

Contents

Webster's New World
Guide To
Punctuation

INTRODUCTION

Punctuate: Medieval Latin
punctuare, to mark
with a point; from
Latin *punctum*, pricked
mark, point; from the
past participle of
pungere, to prick or
pierce.

The purpose of punctuation is to make writing clear. Since punctuation clarifies the meaning and relationships between groups of words, a sound knowledge of grammar is necessary for its mastery.

In most businesses and professions, punctuation is considered a trivial matter, often left to the judgment of clerks and secretaries. But in the law, a misplaced comma can literally mean the difference between life and death. In business, too, a misplaced comma can change the entire meaning of a letter or contract.

Thus "to mark with a point"—or punctuation—is a vital tool in accurate, clear communication.

Most scholars attribute the invention of punctuation to Aristophanes of Byzantium, who was in charge of the great library of Alexandria *circa* 194 B.C. He invented a system of points that corresponded to our comma, semicolon, and period to mark short, medium, and long periods of writing.

In addition, Aristophanes is credited with inventing other punctuation and accent marks. He is said to have invented the virgule, hyphen, apostrophe, and question mark.

As originally conceived by Aristophanes, the hyphen, used to denote compound words, was drawn as a curve or a line *under* the appropriate letters. Between Aristophanes and the Renaissance, the history of punctuation showed two important developments. Lower case letters began to be used (where formerly all capital letters had been the custom), and the *ascenders* and *descenders* of these lower case letters made it harder to read a manuscript without punctuation.

Charlemagne, King of the Franks from 768 to 814 and Holy Roman Emperor for the latter part of this period, and Alcuin, the English director of his palace school, led an educational revival that produced superior spelling and punctuation in texts. Only a simplified version of Aristophanes's system was used, however. It consisted or two marks: the full point, or the period, and the colon, the latter being used to indicate an intermediate stop.

By the 11th century, Aristophanes's full system was in use. New marks, including the *punctus interrogativus* which resembled today's question mark, were introduced. Thus, our modern marks of punctuation were originally divisions in the structure of a sentence derived from Greek grammar.

Incidentally, the first punctuation—vertical lines between phrases—can be seen on the Moonbite stone, dating from 850 B.C. The Semitic script recounts King Moab's war on the Israelites, according to author Robert Claiborne in *The Birth of Writing*.

Modern punctuation can be loosely traced back to Aldus Manutius, a sixteenth-century Venetian printer who did not *invent* punctuation but is generally given the credit for systematizing it. Other printers adopted Manutius's usage and added marks of their own.

The actual history of punctuation is beclouded except for the work that Aristophanes and Manutius did. Manuscripts dating back as far as the fourth century B.C. have rudimentary pointing. In the earliest stone inscriptions, a dot is sometimes placed after every word to separate it from the one following. The modern use of the period as a complete stop evolved roughly in the eighth century A.D. The comma at first looked exactly like the number seven (7), then slowly evolved into a slash mark or virgule (/) and eventually became altered to its present form.

The question mark evolved out of the semicolon. Early printers substituted an upright comma over a period for the semicolon because the latter broke the alignment of their type, thus inventing the question mark. But just about everything about early punctuation is speculation. The only thing certain about its history is that it developed in a casual, random fashion as printing improved, and printers copied, adopted, and adapted, adding their own variations as they worked.

Here is a fascinating example of punctuation, *circa* 1525. It is from Bancke's *Herball*, an early botanical and medical book. The only known original copies are in the Huntington Library in Pasadena, California and the British Museum.

> This herbe is hote and dry/take the flowres and put them in a lynen clothe/ & fo boyle them in fayre clene water to e halfe & coole it & drynke it/for it is moche worth agaynft all euylles in the body. Alfo take the flowres & make powder thereof and bynde it to the ryght arme in a lynen clothe/ & it fhall make the lyght and mery.

Note the use of the slash mark or virgule which serves as a comma. Also note that the period was in use at this time, and the liberal use of ampersands. It's interesting to see that "the" is printed "e." If you substitute "s" for the letter "f" in the above paragraph, you can make some sense out of it since "agaynft" will become "agaynst," a quaint way of spelling "against." That strange word "euylles," of course, is "ills."

The purpose of punctuation is to promote clarity of expression. This famous trick sentence beautifully illustrates this point.

> Jones where Smith had had had had had had had had had had had the examiners approval.

By adding some simple punctuation, we can clarify the sentence:

> Jones, where Smith had had "had," had had "had had." "Had had" had had the examiner's approval.

Today, the trend is towards *less* punctuation rather than more. In his book *Punctuate it Right*

(Barnes & Noble Books, 1983), author Harry Shaw reports a study done on the *American Monthly* magazine. In 1911, the magazine used 310 marks of punctuation in a study of 100 sentences. By 1981, the publication's 100 sentences used 252. Similarly, studies conducted by the *New York Times* and *Harper's* magazine show declines in the use of punctuation. Unnecessary commas (those not needed to make a sentence's meaning clear) are being eliminated. Many writers and editors are eliminating the final comma in a sentence containing a series of items such as "Mary went to the store and bought bread, milk, carrots, and butter." Today, the three commas in the first sentence of Lincoln's *Gettysburg Address* would probably be eliminated:

> Four score and seven years ago our fathers brought forth on this continent, a new nation, conceived in Liberty, and dedicated to the proposition that all men are created equal.

Before you break the rules, however, you must be thoroughly familiar with them. And most editors would rather you err on the side of the angels and include that last comma before the "and" in any sentence containing a list. If the editor wishes, s/he can remove it. Until told otherwise, it's best to include it. Here are the rules you need to know . . .

SO YOU THINK PUNCTUATION DOESN'T MATTER

> Mary Queen of Scots was walking and talking
> a half hour after her head was cut off.

Quite an unusual feat, wouldn't you say?
Let's try adding some punctuation:

> Mary, Queen of Scots, was walking and talk-
> ing; a half hour after, her head was cut off.

Here is an example of a comma changing the meaning of a sentence:

The play ended happily.	(The play had a happy ending!)
The play ended, happily.	(The bored audience was pleased when the play came to an end.)

Here, an apostrophe makes all the difference:

A wise dog knows its master.	(This dog recognizes its owner.)
A wise dog knows it's master.	(This dog clearly knows it has the upper hand . . . er, ah . . . paw.)

The children in this parade are clearly overburdened:

In the parade will be several hundred children carrying flags and many important officials.

By adding a comma the matter is clarified:

In the parade will be several hundred children carrying flags, and many important officials.

In this first example the senate group is clearly cannibalistic:

The senate group eats chickens, cabinet wives, pork chops.

Let's add a semicolon:

The senate group eats chickens; cabinet wives, pork chops.

A comma makes all the difference:

The Democrats, say the Republicans, are sure to win the 1990 election.

Without the commas the sentence has an entirely different meaning:

The Democrats say the Republicans are sure to win the 1990 election.

An apostrophe changes an insulting butler into a figure of perfect decorum:

The butler stood at the door and called the guests names.
Contrast:
The butler stood at the door and called the guests' names.

Which sentence is an insult?

What's the latest dope? What's the latest, dope?

Which sentence is insulting to women?

Thirteen girls knew the secret, all told.
Thirteen girls knew the secret; all told.

Is he a fool or not?

I left him convinced he was a fool.
I left him, convinced he was a fool.

Which headline is libelous?

Population of New York Broken Down by Age
and Sex
Population of New York, Broken Down by Age
and Sex

Was the chicken fried or what?

Michael ate a half-fried chicken.
Michael ate a half fried chicken.

Which scientist is not frightened?

What great scientist recently wrote an article
beginning, "I am frightened"?
What great scientist recently wrote an article
beginning, "I am frightened?"

THE PERIOD

> **Period:** Dot: From Middle
> English *dot*
> (unattested), lump dot;
> from Old English *dott*,
> head of a boil.

The period, or full stop as the British say, is an important mark of punctuation. Do not denigrate it as so simple to comprehend that it is not worth time or study.

A small dot can make a big difference as Philip Howard relates in his book, *The State of the Language* (Oxford University Press, New York, 1985). Howard cites a telegram sent to Dr. Leander Starr Jameson in the Transvaal at the time of an uprising of "uitlanders" in 1895. It read, without punctuation:

> It is under these circumstance that we feel constrained to call upon you to come to our aid should a disturbance arise here the circumstances are so extreme that we cannot but believe that you and the men under you will not fail to come to the rescue of people who are so situated.

The meaning of the telegram depends upon where you put a period. If you put it after "here," the telegram becomes a conditional invitation. If you put it after "aid," the telegram is a direct invitation to come at once. Either way, it didn't affect history.

Jameson led his raid anyway. During troubles in Johannesburg between Uitlanders and the Boer government, he led the famous Jameson Raid, an attempt to cross the Transvaal to take help to the Uitlanders in Johannesburg. He was forced to surrender to General Cronje in January, 1896. Handed over by President Kruger to British authorities for trial, he was sent to England and imprisoned.

Use a period after a complete declarative sentence:

A single woman's social life is perilous.
I often feel as though I'm cast adrift in an open sea in a leaky life boat.
I meet charismatic philanderers wherever I go.

Other Uses for the Period

Use a period after an indirect question:

He asked me if I could stay after school.
The boss wanted to know when I would have the report completed.
Please tell me what she said about her vacation plans.

A question mark after any of these sentences would distort the meaning and confuse the reader.

A direct question is followed by a question mark, of course. And a direct command usually requires an exclamation point. However, a question or command may be so mild in its phrasing that a period is more commonly used:

Please have your report in on time.
Please drop by for a visit some day.
May we please have a prompt reply.

Use a period after abbreviations:

Dr.	Sr.	i.e.	Esq.
Capt.	Jr.	e.g.	Pres.
doz.	LL.D.	Rev.	P.S.
Mrs.	pp.	Lt.	R.S.V.P.
Co.	etc.	Sgt.	O.E.D.

As a rule, we do not use periods after the letters representing well-known organizations such as a government agency, network call letters, acronyms, or radio/TV stations:

ASCAP	NATO	SHAPE	CIA
UNESCO	RAP	UNICEF	FBI
NBC	BBC	FHA	FDA
TV	WASP	CBS	IBM
WAVES	YUPPIE	ABC	AT&T
AWOL	WNEW	POW	TB

Use no periods after chemical symbols, even though they are abbreviations:

O (oxygen)	B (boron)	Cu (copper)
H_2O (water)	Ca (calcium)	Kr (krypton)
Fe (iron)	Ma (magnesium)	Sn (tin)
Bi (bismuth)	Cr (chromium)	Zn (zinc)

Do not use periods after trigonometric terms:

cos	cot	mod	tan
coses	log	sin	

Do not use periods after chess terms:

K   B   Q   Kt   Kh3   Bh5   Kd4   Ke3   Kxe3

NOTE: The French use no period after an abbreviation. The practice is seldom followed in this country, but should be noted.

FRENCH FORM	ENGLISH FORM
Mme	Mme.
Cie	Cie.
Mlle	Mlle.

Shortened forms of words are not considered abbreviations and do not require a period:

exam	math	auto
gym	taxi	photo
lab	percent	ad

Abbreviated forms of names require periods:

Chas.	Jos.
Jas.	Wm.
Thos.	Eliz.

Shortened forms of names, however, do not require a period.

Jim	Tom	Liz
Sam	Nell	Alex
Will	Joe	Pete

Use no periods after ordinal numbers when written thus:

1st	He served in the 5th battalion.
2nd	Please see me after 1st period.
3rd, etc.	She belonged to the 3rd group.

If a declarative sentence ends with a period, use only one period. In the examples below, the period in the abbreviations "Mass." ends the sentence. Therefore, do not add another period:

INCORRECT: She lived in Brookline, Mass. .
CORRECT: She lived in Brookline, Mass.

Inside a sentence, an abbreviation using a period is followed with any other required punctuation marks:

You say he comes from Santa Monica, Calif.; I wonder if that's true!
He says he was raised in Boston, Mass.—nonsense, his accent disputes it!

Use a period after numbers or letters which enumerate an outline:

1. PUNCTUATION
   A. Period
   B. Comma
   C. Colon
   D. Semicolon

Use a period after initials in proper names:

John D. Rockefeller
Robert L. Stevenson

But not after initials which identify a prominent person:

LBJ
JFK
FDR

If parentheses intervene in a sentence, a period is used after the abbreviation, as well as to end the sentence:

> The lecture will begin at 9 A.M. (not 9 P.M.).
> Please start at 7 A.M. (and not 8 A.M. as originally planned).

Use no periods after Roman numerals (except when they end a sentence):

> She liked the style of furniture used by Louis XIV.
> There have been XXII Super Bowls to date.
> Louis XIV's palace is very lavish.
> Please read chapter VII in your Latin book.
> Louis XVIII's full name was Louis Xavier Stanislas, and he was sometimes called Louis le Desiré. He was the grandson of Louis XV and brother of Louis XVI and Charles X.
> George VI succeeded Edward VIII as King of England.

The Period Fault

Don't use a period after what is logically as well as grammatically a fragment of a sentence, such as a phrase or a subordinate clause. This usage is called the "period fault." For example:

CORRECT:	My aunt has moved to Los Angeles, where she plans to go into the fashion business.
INCORRECT:	My aunt has moved to Los Angeles. Where she plans to go into the fashion business.
CORRECT:	He entered the house, leaving the back door open for a hasty exit.

INCORRECT:	He entered the house. Leaving the back door open for a hasty exit.
CORRECT:	She had one immediate ambition, to study drama and go to Hollywood.
INCORRECT:	She had one immediate ambition. To study drama and go to Hollywood.

Do not use a period after a title when it is the closing of a letter:

INCORRECT	CORRECT
Sincerely.	Sincerely,
George Higgins.	George Higgins
General Manager.	General Manager

THE QUESTION MARK

Question Mark: From Latin,
feminine past
participle of
quaerere, to seek.

The question mark, or interrogation point, indicates an expression of inquiry, uncertainty, or doubt.

Use a question mark after every direct question:

What time does the movie start?
Can you be here by 8 o'clock?
Where did you go on vacation?

Some writers prefer to use only one question mark when a series of questions falls within a single sentence. However, formal usage dictates the following:

The five questions of journalism are *Who?*
Where? Why? When? And *How?* Who won the
prize? Was it Sally? Ben? or John?

Do not use a question mark after indirect questions:

She asked how tall John was.
Marlon wondered why.
How to live until graduation—that is the
essential question for Sabrina.

The difference between an *indirect* and *direct* question may be minimal.

DIRECT: It is wise to ask, "How many months
before Sabrina graduates?"

INDIRECT: It is wise to ask how many months
before Sabrina graduates.

Use a question mark enclosed in parentheses to indicate uncertainty:

He was born in 1898 (?) and died in 1930.
Shakespeare was born on April 23 (?), 1564.
During the summer, a pair of mockingbirds (?)
built a nest in the tree next to my office
window.

Use a question mark enclosed in parentheses to indicate humor or irony:

Our food was dropped from the air which
tenderized (?) the meat.
I found the beauty queen to be very modest (?)
and unassuming.

A question mark should be placed inside the quotation marks when it is part of a quotation and outside if it is not part of the quotation:

Have you seen the television miniseries "Elvis
and Me"?
Alfred E. Neuman's favorite expression is,
"What, me worry?"

Even though the question mark is considered a terminal (end of sentence) mark, it may appear elsewhere in the sentence:

Who will go to the airport with me? John? Sally?
Mark? No one?

Is it time to go? When? Where? To the station or
to the airport?
Whose sweater is this? Is it Heather's? Russell's?
Or is it John's?

With requests, a period is used, not a question mark:

Will you please return my library book.
Will you close the door.
As you read, will you write down every word
you don't understand.

However, these sentences may be intended as *questions* rather than *statements* and, in that case, could easily take a question mark:

Will you please return my library book?
Will you close the door?
Will you write down every word you don't
understand?
Will the audience please rise as we sing "The
Star Spangled Banner"?

The Question Mark with Other Marks

With quotation marks and parentheses:

If the question mark *is part of the quoted
material*, it goes *inside* the quotation marks. If it is
not part of the quoted material, it belongs outside
the quotations:

"Will we sail on time?" he asked.
"Do we arrive at 8 A.M.?" she queried.
Why did she say, "Your souvenirs are too
expensive"?
Isn't it true that sometimes we say, "The devil
with the schedule"?

With a comma:

If a question mark falls within a sentence where logically a comma is desired, *omit the comma*. No confusion results.

> Our travel schedule is clarified when we consider that the questions what time? when? and where? are all answered in the printed brochure.

With a period:

When a question mark (or an exclamation point) ends a sentence, *omit the period*. Thus:

> Did she say, "I want to move to England"?

THE EXCLAMATION POINT

Exclamation Point: From Old
French
Exclamer; from
Latin
exclamare, to
call out,
exclaim

The exclamation point is like a flash of lightning in a dark sky. It cries out, calls for attention, and emphasizes. But it should be used *sparingly.* Many amateur writers lean on the exclamation point to make it do all the work of lending importance to their work, when the words themselves should bear the brunt of the work. An exclamation point will not add verve or élan to colorless and boring prose. Only use an exclamation point for added force when appropriate. A good rule to follow is never to use an exclamation point when another mark of punctuation will do. Closely adhered to, this rule will keep you from sprinkling your words with "gushy" phrases and marks and lend the judiciously used exclamation point its proper importance.

The exclamation point is legitimately used to express strong emotion:

I hate it!
He's disgusting!

What a nasty thing to say!
What an idiot you are!

The exclamation point is used to command:

Do it at once!
Get moving now, just as fast you can!
Don't touch me again!
Get out of my way!

The exclamation mark can be used to express irony or sarcasm:

"What a beautiful day!" she exclaimed as she
opened her umbrella.
"So what!" he exclaimed.
Since our labor board's negotiations went so
smoothly, we'll just have to call a general strike!

NOTE: Do not overuse the exclamation mark to
express sarcasm. It is always obtrusive, and its
overuse becomes labored. Use it occasionally, always bearing in mind that the words you choose to
express your point should bear the main weight of
the message.

An exclamation point is often used after strong interjections:

Olé!   Encore!
Bravo!   Hooray!
Hurrah! Wow!

Mild interjections such as *drat, ouch, oh, so,
indeed,* or *well* can usually be followed by a

comma, depending upon the degree of emotion you wish to convey.

An exclamation point is placed *inside* parentheses when it belongs with the text enclosed:

> Tom says he won't go to the prom (he hates dancing!), so I will go with Russell.
> Mary is afraid of spiders (what a silly phobia!), but I am not frightened of them at all.

An exclamation point is placed *inside* quotation marks when it is part of the matter which is quoted:

> "I hate dancing!" he exclaimed, "so I won't go to the prom."
> "What a silly phobia!" I told Mary when she said she was afraid of spiders.

The exclamation point goes *outside* both parentheses and quotation marks when it is not part of the text enclosed in parentheses or part of the quotation:

> Tom says he won't go to the prom (he hates dancing), so I will go with Russell!
> Mary's phobia (she hates spiders) is so silly!

THE SEMICOLON

Semicolon: From Latin *semi*, "half"
a half of a *kolon* or limb.

Up until about a century ago, the semicolon and colon were used interchangeably. But they have distinctive uses today. *Semi*, of course, means *half*. So, literally, the semicolon describes itself as a half of a colon. Its function today is as *half a period* or a demoted period. It doesn't bring a sentence to a complete stop, as a period does, but it has a stronger meaning than a comma. Many people never conquer the use of a semicolon, and yet the rules which govern its uses are quite simple, and it can be an extremely effective mark of punctuation.

A semicolon is used to separate two main or independent clauses that are not joined by a coordinated conjunction such as *and, but, for, or, nor,* **and** *yet:*

> The abstract art was removed from the company's hallways; realistic pictures of sunsets and landscapes were hung in its place.
> Horror movies are all the rage; a particular moneymaker is *Friday the 13th.*

Be careful not to use semicolons to set off phrases or dependent clauses. Setting off dependent clauses or phrases will only serve to confuse rather than clarify:

> INCORRECT: Since Barbara is very meticulous; we
> have to be careful with our
> details.

My purpose is; to succeed at
tennis.
CORRECT: Since Barbara is very meticulous, we
have to be careful with our details.
My purpose is to succeed at tennis.

A comma is not strong enough to mark the break between two independent clauses. Instead, a semicolon or period is needed.

When only a comma is used, we have a *comma splice*, or *comma fault:*

CORRECT: Wear your boots; it's snowing. Let's
get up; it's morning.
INCORRECT: Wear your boots, it's snowing. Let's
get up, it's morning.

A semicolon should be used to clarify items in a long and complex series:

Most of my family attended the reunion. There
was Mary, my grandmother; Harry, my mother's
cousin; Sally Lou, my second cousin; Margaret,
my aunt; Samantha, my great-great-grandmother;
and lastly Uncle Todd.
You will need to transport the tent, the orange
one with green stripes; the portable stove, which
is kept in the hall closet; the cooler, which Bob
gave us last year; the blankets, stored in the
attic; and lots of food.

A semicolon is used before a conjunctive adverb which separates two main clauses:

The most common conjunctive adverbs are
*accordingly, also, anyhow, besides, consequently,
furthermore, hence, however, in addition, indeed,*

likewise, moreover, nevertheless, still, then, and *therefore:*

> Michael failed his admissions exam;
> consequently, he won't be attending the university.
> I was late getting to the audition; anyhow, I
> didn't want to be in the play.
> My boss gave me a healthy raise; in addition,
> he's giving me two days off next week.
> He is an effective, likable speaker; moreover, he
> makes a good appearance.

A semicolon should be used to separate items in a series which contains other punctuation:

> His sales calls took him to St. Joseph, Missouri;
> Salt Lake City, Utah; Carson City, Nevada;
> Virginia City, Nevada; and finally to Los Angeles.

The semicolon should be placed outside the quotation or parentheses. When the matter quoted ends with a semicolon, the semicolon is dropped:

> Michael assumed everyone had read "Leda And
> The Swan"; he referred to it many times during
> the class discussion.
> Michael hoped the editors would read the
> manuscript before the weekend (several of them
> had promised that they would); but by Monday,
> he still didn't have a decision.

THE COLON

Colon: From Latin *colon,*
units of verse; from
Greek, *kolon,* "limb."

A colon placed within a sentence indicates that the words after the colon are connected in some way or equal to the words preceding the colon.

The colon is used after the salutation in a formal or business letter:

Dear Sir: Dear Governor Brown: Dear Mr.
Throckmorton:

Meanwhile, a comma is used in an informal letter:

Dear Honeybunch,   Dearest Susie,   Dear Mom,

The colon is commonly used to introduce a list or series:

California's traffic study included the three most
critical areas: Los Angeles, the San Fernando
Valley, and Glendale.

He has written many books: *A Child's Garden of
Verses, Treasure Island, Kidnapped, Dr. Jekyll
and Mr. Hyde, The Black Arrow, The Merry
Men,* and many, many more.

Do not use a colon before a brief, casual series:

INCORRECT: The school subjects I like best are:
English, literature, and journalism.

26

CORRECT: The school subjects I like best are English, literature, and journalism.

A colon is used before a clause that is a restatement, illustration, or explanation:

Fitzgerald once quarreled with Hemingway: the latter had made a disparaging remark about him in one of his books.
Laurence Peter believes that laughter can keep you well: his books are crammed with one-liners, quips, and prescriptions for laughter.

The colon is used to introduce a formal statement, an extract, or a speech in dialogue:

The rule is stated thus: "Always . . .
This is a direct quote from his speech: "The time has come to . . .
MICHAEL: Haven't you finished that chapter yet?
AURIEL: I only have three more pages to do.

A colon is used between hours and minutes when indicating time:

It is now 11:30 A.M.
Please attend the 3:30 meeting.

A colon is used between chapter and verse in scriptural passages:

Matt., 2:5–13

A colon is used between volume and page references:

Los Angeles Times, Vol. 1:16

The colon is placed outside quotation marks or parentheses:

I have three reasons for liking the song "Good Year for the Roses": metaphorical originality, haunting melody, and the note of sadness in Elvis Costello's voice.

THE COMMA

Comma: Latin, from Greek
komma, that which is cut
off, section, clause; from
koptein, to cut

The comma, the most frequently used puncutation mark, is also the mark which is most apt to give you trouble.

> A famous author was complaining bitterly to his friends about his difficult day at the typewriter.
>
> "What did you do all day?" they asked curiously.
>
> He shook his head as though to clear his thoughts. "In the morning, I inserted a comma in my manuscript," he replied, "and in the afternoon, I took it out."
>
> His admiring comrades promptly bought him another stiff drink.

Arguments break out about commas. Copy editors make wagers on the accuracies of their comma placements. Editorial offices bristle between pro-comma advocates and anti-comma advocates. The former put commas wherever they can, sprinkling them lavishly as though from an inexhaustible supply. Anti-comma people use them judiciously and rid their sentences of every unnecessary one. If you read prose written and published

100 years ago, you will notice that the tendency has been away from the overuse of the comma. Today, there are definite principles that guide its use. The principle apt to trap even the most alert is that spelled out in the *restrictive* and *nonrestrictive* rules outlined below. A few minutes absorbing these principles will be a few minutes well spent.

How delicious to be able to say to the office know-it-all, "Excuse me, Rasmussen, unless I miss my guess, you have two misplaced commas in your otherwise exquisitely-written and relentlessly forthright memo on office overtime. See, you've mistaken a restrictive clause for a nonrestrictive clause."

Between Main Clauses

A comma separates independent clauses joined by a coordinating conjunction (*as, and, but, or, nor, for*):

> I was determined to know Joel better, and I devised a plan.
> I would plan an evening at home, but first, I'd have to improve my cooking skills.

Commas are also used to separate clauses *not* joined by conjunctions:

> I discussed my plans with my best friend, Melissande, who was very enthusiastic.

With Compound Predicates

Commas are not usually used to separate the parts of a compound predicate:

CORRECT:	I reasoned and decided to know him better.
INCORRECT:	I reasoned, and decided, to know him better.
CORRECT:	I filled my days with dreams of the perfect evening together and spent my evenings searching for the perfect recipe.
INCORRECT:	I filled my days with dreams of the perfect evening together, and spent my evenings searching for the perfect recipe.

With Subordinate Clauses and Phrases

Phrases that precede a main clause with adverbial clauses are usually set off with commas.

As I get older, I tend to worry about my future.
When I made the decision, I turned my thoughts to a romantic tryst.
When you understand the importance I placed on the evening, you will also know quite a bit about me (and my insecurity).
As it is seen from a bookkeeper's perspective, my daily view is a plateau of paper.

Do not use a comma between parallel subordinate clauses joined by *and, but, for, nor,* or *or,* unless clarity demands It:

As I get older and as I tend to worry about my future, I despair.
If you understand the importance I placed on the evening, and since it is necessary to know a little about me, let me tell you more.

With Appositives

Set off any nouns, with their modifiers, when used in apposition to another noun:

> Melissande Applebaum, the assistant bookkeeper, has a very successful social life.
> Melissande, my best friend, has a polished worldliness that I envy.

In apposition means a word or group of words which follows a noun or pronoun and means or stands for the same thing as the noun or pronoun. For example, in the first sentence above, the words *the assistant bookkeeper* are in apposition to the noun, *Melissande Applebaum*, and help explain it. In the second sentence, *my best friend* is in apposition to *Melissande*.

With Introductory Words and Words That Interrupt

Commas set off words such as *finally, meanwhile, however, after all,* and *especially* when they begin a sentence as well as words which interrupt a sentence:

> Indeed, you might say Melissande is a role model for me.
> I am eager to learn her social and dating skills; however, I have some thoughts of my own on the subject.
> She believes I should serve steak on the night of Joel's visit; however, I feel that choice is too common.

With Contrasting Expressions

A comma is used to set off contrasting expressions within a sentence:

> Melissande is of the belief that a romance must be established over many weeks, not in one evening.
>
> Sometimes her advice, although eminently realistic, is a bit on the negative side.

Adjectives and adverbs that modify the same word or phrase and that are joined by *but* or another coordinating conjunction (*either, or, neither, nor,* etc.) do not require a comma:

> Tall and handsome Joel entered the room.
> The very tall and extremely beautiful woman saw Joel.

Items in a Series

Words, clauses, and phrases joined in a series are separated by commas:

> Champagne, roast chicken, mashed potatoes, salad, fruit, and cheese comprise my chosen menu.

NOTE: The use of the comma after the last item, *fruit,* is omitted by many grammarians but recommended and used by others for explicit clarity.

A comma is not used to separate items in a series that are joined by conjunctions:

> Champagne and roast chicken and mashed potatoes plus salad or fruit and cheese comprise my menu.

NOTE: When the items in a series are long (usually more than three) and complicated, the use of a semicolon may be preferable to that of a comma.

With Compound Modifiers

A comma is used to separate *two or more* adjectives or adverbs or phrases that modify the same word or phrase:

> My plans for an intriguing, romantic interlude were taking concrete shape.
> Melissande scrutinized my shopping list with an approving, appreciative air.
> I feel confident, exhilarated.

A comma is *not* used between two adjectives when their combination modifies a word or phrase.

CORRECT: An art nouveau apartment will be the site.
             Light blue candles will adorn my table.
             A white lace tablecloth will enhance the scene.
INCORRECT: A small, modern apartment . . . Tall, blue candles . . . A white, lace . . .

CHECKPOINT: A good method to determine this usage is to ask if the word *and* can be inserted between the two modifiers without changing the meaning of the sentence. If it cannot, no comma is required.

Use a comma between words repeated for effect:

> I am beginning to feel excited, excited, excited.
> Joel, Joel, Joel, I can think of no one else.
> I am very, very pleased with my stratagems so far.

Parenthetical Items

Set off a word, phrase, or clause serving as an aside or digression—which interrupts sharply the even flow of a sentence—with commas. (The writer's judgment must determine whether the item in question breaks the even flow enough to justify commas.)

To be truthful about it, my long-awaited evening was a disaster.
Joel ate like a pig, I must confess, devouring my gourmet meal like a swine.
He also pointedly rejected my cat's loving overtures in a gross fashion, ignoring Sweetpea's adoring importunings to be petted.
To be blunt about it, his manner is irritating.
Football, with all its impossible ramifications, is his only subject of conversation.
I faced, moreover, an exhausting clean-up job the next morning.
My social evenings, for the time being, will be devoted to bowling.

Transitional Adverbs

Transitional adverbs such as *however, moreover, nevertheless, therefore, too, also,* etc., produce a strong parenthetical effect:

Furthermore, he prefers steak to chicken.
I shall, therefore, spend future evenings alone.

Use commas to set off nonrestrictive clauses and phrases:

Our newest boat, which is painted red and white, has sprung a leak.

James Lee, who owns this bank and five others,
is one of the wealthiest men in the state.
Joe Doe, who is handsome, friendly, and
courteous, is exceedingly stupid.
Catherine Jones, the club president, is a very
active woman.
Elizabeth Jones, her sister, is quite shy.
This, my friends, is the whole truth.

Non-restrictive means that without the clause,
the same point would be made. Judgment comes
into play here. For example, would the first sentence above mean the same thing if the phrase
which is painted red and white were removed? Yet
it would. It would still make its main point which
is that our newest boat has sprung a leak. That it is
painted red and white is irrelevant to the meaning
of the sentence. Therefore, the phrase is set off
with commas.

Restrictive clauses and phrases do not require commas.

In each of the following illustrations, the sentence
would be quite different without the clause or
phrase:

He spent hours caring for the Indian guides who
were sick with malaria.

(He didn't just care for the Indian guides; he cared
for only those who were sick with malaria.)

The car parked across the street is ready.

(It's a specific car. It's the one which is parked across the street.)

A boat that leaks is of little use.

(No one can dispute this remark. But take out *that leaks* and your sentence means something entirely different. This is a restricted phrase. It cannot be removed without changing the meaning of the sentence. Therefore, no commas are required.)

Incorrect Usage of the Comma

To be heartily avoided is the way many writers as well as editors sprinkle commas throughout material as though they had a shaker filled with commas, instead of salt.

As Gertrude Stein said, "Commas are servile and they have no life of their own." To take their proper servile position, commas need a master. Modern punctuation tends to *omit* many commas that were formerly used. Reputable writers and editors do deviate from the rules upon occasion, but their deviations *do not establish new principles.* Here are some examples where the use of a comma is entirely unnecessary:

1. Do not use a comma before the *first* or after the *last* word in a series:

CORRECT: Iced coffee is a cold, sweet, refreshing drink on a hot day.

INCORRECT: Iced coffee is a, cold, sweet, refreshing, drink on a hot day.

2. Do not use a comma to separate a subject from its predicate. No commas are needed in the following sentences:

I asked that the stoplights be installed on the corner.
I quickly discerned exactly what type of person he was.
The Eastern visitors found the California climate too warm.

3. Do not use a comma between two independent clauses where a strong mark of punctuation is indicated. As mentioned earlier, this misuse is often called *the comma fault* or *comma splice.* It always causes confusion. A period or semicolon is clearly called for in the following sentence:

INCORRECT: The boss asked me to work late, I
             told him I could not.
CORRECT: The boss asked me to work late; I
             told him I could not.
CORRECT: The boss asked me to work late. I
             told him I could not.

4. There is no disagreement among grammarians about whether or not to use a pair of commas with words in apposition which are nonrestrictive. The underlined words in the following sentences identify, describe, define, or limit.

INCORRECT: My brother <u>Daniel</u> is an excellent
             typist.
CORRECT: My brother, <u>Daniel,</u> is an excellent
             typist.

38

INCORRECT:	Shakespeare's play _As You Like It_ is one of my favorites.
CORRECT:	Shakespeare's play, _As You Like It,_ is one of my favorites.
INCORRECT:	Eleanor of Aquitaine was the mother of Richard the Lion-Hearted.
CORRECT:	Eleanor, of Aquitaine, was the mother of Richard, the Lion-Hearted.

5. Do not use a comma indiscriminately to replace a word or group of words which are omitted. Occasionally, it can take the place of pronouns such as _that, who, whom,_ or _which,_ but constant use becomes tedious:

INCORRECT:	Barbara promised, she would visit me soon.
CORRECT:	Barbara promised that she would visit me soon.
INCORRECT:	The professor, I saw at the library was an old friend.
CORRECT:	The professor whom I saw at the library was an old friend.
INCORRECT:	She thought, that girl was brilliant.
CORRECT:	She thought that that girl was brilliant.

6. On most occasions, you eliminate the second comma in firm names such as:

INCORRECT:	Sloan, Field, & Company
CORRECT:	Sloan, Field & Company
INCORRECT:	Vegetable, Greengrocers, & Growers Association
CORRECT:	Vegetable, Greengrocers & Growers Association

39

PARENTHESES

Parentheses: Late Latin, from Greek, "a putting in beside"; from *parentithenai*, to insert; *para*, beside.

Parentheses around a group of words within a sentence indicate that these words are not essential to the meaning of the sentence.

Words contained in parentheses often bear no direct grammatical resemblance to the rest of the sentence.

Use parentheses to enclose incidental material which is considered unimportant:

Consigned to which, and to a speedy end (for mental torture is not supportable beyond a certain point, and that point I feel I have attained), my course is run.

Undulating hills were changed to valleys, undulating valleys (with a solitary storm bird sometimes skimming through them) were lifted up to hills.

Senator McGuire (D., Oregon) is chairman of the committee.

Company sales in the products' division have soared (see Graph B), and we hope will continue to rise throughout the spring.

The musical comedy lyrics (see p. 83) are very clever.

Use parentheses to enclose numerals or letters marking divisions or enumerations in the text:

He assigned homework in the following classes: (1) History, (2) Mathematics, (3) Spelling. Parentheses are used to distinguish (a) explanatory material, (b) material of less importance, (c) divisions in the text.

Punctuation marks are used within parentheses when they belong with the parenthetical material. They are placed outside the parentheses when they belong with the main part of the sentence:

Let's invite Allyson (is that the way she spells her name?) to the party.
Did you invite Allyson (does she spell her name that way?) to the party?

Parentheses are used to enclose bibliographical data or historical data set off from the text:

Martin Chuzzlewit (1858) was one of Dickens' darker novels.
Mary I or Mary Tudor (often called *Bloody Mary*) was Queen of England and Ireland from 1553–58.

Parentheses set off cross references:

This book is available at our East Coast stores (see p. 24 for complete list).

THE APOSTROPHE

Apostrophe: From Latin
apostrophe; from
Greek, *apostrephein,*
to run away.

The apostrophe is another troublesome mark of punctuation, and yet, a moment or two spent studying its rules will show that they are really very simple.

An apostrophe indicates the place (or space) where letters have been omitted in a contraction. A contraction is a word made up of two words combined into one by omitting one or more letters such as:

don't/do not
it's/it is
they're/they are

NOTE: A common error is to insert an apostrophe in the possessive form *its* which requires none. Only when you want to substitute *it is* with a contraction is an apostrophe required. Another careless mistake is to put the apostrophe in the wrong place: do'nt or does'nt. Careful attention to apostrophes will soon make you their master.

No apostrophe is required when using the possessive form of *its*:

The cat was chasing its tail.
The horse was in its stall.
The baby played with its rattle.

An apostrophe is required when using the contraction for *it is:*

It's too late to go out.
It's a long way to Tipperary.

HINT: Read your sentence silently to yourself, and if you are using a contraction of "It is . . ." your sentence requires an apostrophe (It's). You wouldn't say, "The cat was chasing it is tail," would you? Again, with the possessive form of "Its . . ." no apostrophe is required.

Use an apostrophe with "s" to indicate the possessive case of a singular noun or a plural noun not ending in "s":

child's toy
children's dolls
lady's hat
Burns's *Tam O'Shanter*

Charles's reign
his son-in-law's
business
somebody else's pen
one's intentions

For plural nouns that end in "s," add only an apostrophe after the "s":

ladies' hats
Joneses' houses
the Charleses' reigns

elephants' trunks
schools' students
tables' legs

Use an apostrophe to indicate omission of a letter or letters:

I'm sure you're going to enjoy the show.
He didn't mind waiting for her.

43

o'clock (of the clock)
will-o'-the-wisp (will of the wisp)
jack-o'-lantern (Jack of the Lantern)
O'Connor (of Connor)
cont'd. (continued)

Use the apostrophe to show the omission of the century in a date:

He fought through the days of '61–'65.
He graduated in the class of '49.
He fought in the war of '14–'17.
He served a term of office from '82 to '87.

Use the apostrophe to indicate the plural of a figure, letter, or symbol:

Watch your p's and q's.
Be sure to dot your i's and cross your t's.
Does he know his ABC's?
You use too many &'s in your letters.
There are three 1's in your telephone number.

To form the possessive case of a plural noun not ending in "s" add an apostrophe and an "s":

the men's gym
children's games
women's work

Avoid using an apostrophe to form a plural of a noun:

INCORRECT: Truck's and motorcycle's are not
allowed on the freeways.
CORRECT: Trucks and motorcycles are not
allowed on the freeways.

Indefinite pronouns (*one, everyone, everybody*) form their possessive case in the same way as a noun:

Everyone's perception was wrong.
He was angry at everybody's getting a prize.
One's opinions are one's own.
Everybody's license tags will be mailed on the first.

Personal pronouns in the possessive case (*its, ours, yours, theirs, whose, his, her*) do not require an apostrophe:

INCORRECT: I knew the coat was her's.
CORRECT: I knew the coat was hers.
INCORRECT: Do you know who's hat this is?
CORRECT: Do you know whose hat this is?
INCORRECT: Is this your's?
CORRECT: Is this yours?
INCORRECT: You have seen the Broadway theater at it's best.
CORRECT: You have seen the Broadway theater at its best.

The Apostrophe with Compound Words

In hyphenated, compound words, names of business firms, and words showing joint possession, only the last word is possessive in form:

That is my mother-in-law's car.
We like Proctor and Gamble's products.

INCORRECT: We followed the commander's-in-chief orders.
CORRECT: We followed the commander-in-chief's orders.

The apostrophe may be used to make inflected verbs from numerals or letters:

Joe was 86'ed from the beer parlor for
obstreperous behavior.
The champ k.o.'d his opponent in the second
round.

THE ASTERISK

Asterisk: From Greek, *asterikos,*
literally "little star."

The asterisk (*) is a star-shaped character which is
sometimes used to signal a footnote in popular
writing.

At one time the asterisk was also used to indicate
omission of words from a sentence, or from a
paragraph of an even longer piece of writing, but it
has been almost universally abandoned in favor of
ellipsis points.

The asterisk is still sometimes used to suggest the
passage of time in a story. A long line of them
* * * * * * * * * * denotes the end of one episode and the
beginning of the next. But even this usage has
largely given way to ellipsis points or blank space.

Use an asterisk in the following way:

She said she was invited to the dinner* but did
not think she could go.

* The President's Council Dinner at the
California Museum of Science & Industry

If you are using an asterisk to denote a footnote and must use several on the same page, mark the first with one asterisk, the second with two, and the third with three asterisks:

This month's statistics are very impressive.*
His monthly salary** is more than many people
make in a year.
In his new book***, Shad Helmletter obsoletes
current-day motivational methods.

* See chart #17.
** $250,000 per year
*** *What to Say When You Talk to Yourself*

THE HYPHEN

> **Hyphen:** Late Latin from late Greek, *hyphen* or *huyps* meaning under. As originally conceived, the hyphen was drawn *under* compound words.

The surest way to determine if a word should be hyphenated is to use the dictionary. Hyphens show the syllables of a word. For example, the word prac-ti-cal has three syllables and prac-ti-ca-ble has four.

Hyphenate fractions and numbers when used as adjectives before the words they modify:

thirty-three students	But . . . There were thirty three in the class.
a three-fourths majority	But . . . Three fourths of those voting were women.

Hyphenate a compound adjective:

a third-floor apartment	But . . . an apartment on the third floor
an after-school meeting	But . . . a meeting after school
well-planned program	But . . . a program which was well planned

door-to-door soliciting   But . . . soliciting from
                            door to door

**When one of the modifying words is an adverb ending in
-ly, omit the hyphen:**

a beautifully laid table
a nicely prepared speech
a skillfully prepared meal
an artfully conceived presentation

Use a hyphen to prevent confusion or awkward spelling:

re-create	prevents confusion with recreate
re-form	prevents confusion with reform
re-enlist	avoids awkwardness of reenlist
semi-invalid	avoids awkwardness of semiinvalid
re-formation	to distinguish from reformation
re-act	to distinguish from react

**A hyphen is used when a prefix such as *anti, non, pro, un,
ex, self* precedes nouns. A hyphen is also used before the
termination *-elect* with any nouns:**

Un-American	all-star
Pan-American	Governor-elect
pro-Russian	self-styled
inter-Allied	president-elect
ex-governor	chairman-elect

**Capitalize *both parts* of a hyphenated expression if both
parts are proper names (or the equivalent of proper
names):**

The Spanish-American War
The Afro-American Federation
Anglo-American understanding
The Sino-Japanese dispute
The Nazi-Soviet pact

Words beginning with the prefix *non* are written solid unless they are proper nouns:

nonabrasive	noncritical	nonhuman
nonacademic	nondeceptive	noninclusive
nonalcoholic	nondefensive	nonintellectual
nonapplicable	nondomesticated	nonofficial
nonassertive	nondrying	nonpaying
nonbeliever	nonedible	nonrecoverable
nonblooming	nonexclusive	nonsacred
nonbreakable	nonexempt	nonsecular
noncarbonated	nonfactual	nonsparing
noncitizen	nonfatal	nonsubscriber
nonconsent	nonformal	nontechnical
noncontrollable	nonhazardous	nonviolation

But when *non* is used with a proper noun, it is hyphenated:

non-English	non-Japanese
non-Jewish	non-Negro
non-Mormon	non-Moslem
non-Oriental	

NOTE: *non sequitur* (Latin, it does not follow)
       non obstante (Latin, notwithstanding)

Use a hyphen when a capital letter is joined to a noun or to an adjective:

T-square	T-shaped
I-beam	X-ray

| V-necked | U-boat |
| S-curve | U-bolt |

The Hyphen with Compound Words

Of all the questions which arise in an editorial office, one of the most common has to do with compound words. Should it be written taxpayer, tax-payer, or tax payer? Solid, hyphenated, or open? These questions are readily answered by consulting the dictionary. However, there are some general principles that serve to guide:

Definitions

1. *Open* means two words so closely associated as to constitute one unit, such as *stool pigeon*, *high school*, and *settlement house*.

2. *Hyphenated Compound* refers to a combination of words joined by a hyphen, such as *ill-favored* and *fellow-man*.

3. *Solid or Closed Compound* means a combination of two or more words, originally separate, but now spelled as one word, *bookkeeper*, *typesetting*, *notebook*, *schoolteacher*, and *schoolhouse*.

NOTE: Today, the trend in spelling is *away* from the use of the hyphen. There is a preference to spell compounds *solid* as soon as usage and acceptance warrant their being considered permanent compounds. This is a trend, not a rule, but it is helpful to remember that such a trend exists. A final decision must be made by consulting the dictionary.

What is meant by a *permanent compound?* It is

one which has been accepted in general usage and will be found in the dictionary.

bylaws	background
bricklayer	typewriter
battleship	blackboard
fullback	grandfather
proofreader	officeholder

An *impermanent compound* or a *temporary compound* is one that is coined on the spot for the sake of making a point in print:

    a dingy-faced boy
    a diamond-encrusted collar
    a free-form sculpture
    a slow-sailing ship

You will not find dingyfaced, diamondcrusted, freeform, or slowsailing in your dictionary. Compounds such as these require a hyphen.

Hyphenation: Word Division

It is sometimes necessary to divide a word at the end of a printed or typewritten line. These divisions are made between syllables. Determination may be made by consulting the dictionary.

Words should be divided according to *pronunciation:*

    democ-racy (not demo-cracy)
    knowl-edge (not know-ledge)
    antip-odes (not anti-podes)

Words which contain only a silent *e* in the second syllable are never divided:

    aided
    helped

passed
spelled
vexed

Words with a misleading appearance when divided should be left unbroken if at all possible:

CORRECT	INCORRECT
often	of-ten
women	wo-men
prayer	pray-er
noisy	noi-sy

One letter divisions are not acceptable:

u nite   e ven
i tem   a mong
o boe   a men

Two letter divisions are permissible at the end of a line, but two-letter endings should be avoided, if at all possible:

PERMISSIBLE	PREFERABLE
loss-es	losses
mon-ey	money
ful-ly	fully
strick-en	stricken

Compound words such as *court-martial, poverty-stricken, ill-wind, above-mentioned, able-bodied, absent-minded, Anglo-Saxon, bad-tempered* and so forth *should not be broken except at the hyphen if at all possible.* If you break *court-martial,* for instance, into *court-mar-tial,* you will thoroughly confuse your reader. Needless to say, *bad-temp-*

ered or *able-bo-died* creates equally unattractive (not to say curious!) combinations.

The same principle applies to words with pefixes as well such as:

PREFERABLE	PERMISSIBLE
dis-interested	disin-terested
non-refundable	non-re-fundable
pseudo-mechanical	pseudo-mechan-ical

Divide most gerunds and present participles before the *-ing*:

entranc-ing	picnick-ing
learn-ing	whirl-ing
danc-ing	rebuk-ing

Whenever the ending consonant is doubled before the addition of -ing, the added consonant is carried over:

run-ning	dab-bing
trip-ping	abhor-ring
occur-ring	control-ling

Given or surnames of persons ought not to be divided if possible. When initials are used in place of given names, it is permissible (though undesirable) to break after the initials, but extremely poor practice to break between them:

Preferred:	R. L. Stevenson
Permissible:	R. L./Stevenson
Incorrect:	R./L. Stevenson

Abbreviations used with figures should not be separated from the figures:

600 mi.   A.D. 900   7:20 P.M.   16 km.

Review of Hyphenation Rules

Hyphenate all forms of *in-law:*

mother-in-law   father-in-law
brother-in-law   sister-in-law

Hyphenate all *-elect* compounds:

senator-elect
mayor-elect

Hyphenate all fractional numbers:

one-half   three-quarters   two-thirds

Spell temporary compounds with *master* open:

master builder
master mechanic
master chef

Hyphenate compounds with *great-* when discussing relatives:

great-grandfather
great-grandmother
great-aunt

Compounds with *vice-* are best when hyphenated:

vice-chairman   vice-manager
vice-consul   vice-chief

Hyphenate all *self-* compounds:

self-styled   self-hate
self-restrained   self-destructive
self-taught   self-assured
self-loving   self-conscious
self-knowledge

Spell compounds with *ache* solid:

headache   toothache
stomachache   backache

Permanent compounds with *-house* are written solid; temporary compounds are in the main written open:

schoolhouse, boathouse, clubhouse, greenhouse, clearinghouse
EXCEPTIONS: rest house, business house, economics house, fraternity house, sorority house

Permanent compounds with *book* are written solid:

schoolbook, textbook, pocketbook, storybook, notebook
EXCEPTIONS: arithmetic book, reference book, geology book, address book

A phrase used as an adjective before a noun is hyphenated:

up-to-date report	But . . . the report was up to date
matter-of-fact approach	His approach was matter of fact.
how-to-do-it book	This book tells you how to do it.

She gave him the go-ahead; he gave her the run-around.

Was his run-around a put-on?
She found he was playing a cat-and-mouse game.

Hyphenate *all-* compounds before and after a noun:

all-encompassing	all-star	all-time
all-powerful	all-spice	all-out

EXCEPTION: all told

The suffix -like is used to form many compounds. Write them solid unless the words end in a double *l*, or if they are proper nouns:

catlike, floorlike, childlike
EXCEPTIONS: California-like, ball-like, gull-like

THE DASH

Dash: From Middle English
daschen or *dashen*; from
Scandinavian, akin to Danish
daske, "to beat."

The dash conveys panache, élan, and flair to a
sentence. Used with knowledge and judgment, it
becomes one of the most expressive marks in
conveying shades of meaning. The dash can have a
distinctly artistic effect.

One of the most famous uses of the dash is
illustrated in James Thurber's delightful remark
about wine:

> "It's a naive, domestic burgundy—without
> any breeding—but I think you'll be amused
> by its presumption."

A pair of dashes are used to set off insertions, new material, or interpolations in a text that are interruptions:

> Some urge—probably a base one—made me
> giggle.
> Humor results—as I understand it—from the
> juxtaposition of two incongruous ideas.
> We hope this study will explain—not condone—
> the criminal justice system.
> Humor comes from relief of tension—from
> pleasure—in the direct expression of forbidden
> urges.

A dash is used to indicate an unfinished or interrupted statement:

"Everything is funny as long as it is happening to someone else," she said—then she rushed from the table.

Sex is a common source of humor. Are birth control pills deductible?—only if they don't work.

"Why, I wanted the adventure of it, and I'd a waded neck deep in blood too—goodness alive, Aunt Polly!"

A dash is used to set off a final explanatory or summarizing word or statement:

What's it made of—pearls and hammered gold?

To avoid being caught, burglars often commit another crime—murder.

I doled out a double dose of my "alphabet of good health"—the A-to-Z vitamins I thought would assuage my guilt after eating an entire box of chocolate chip cookies.

A dash is used after a quotation to set off the source:

Anybody who goes to see a psychiatrist ought to have his head examined.

—Sam Goldwyn

A verbal contract isn't worth the paper it's written on.

—Sam Goldwyn

But the strangest thing that ever happened to Jim was the time he went boating on Sunday, and didn't get struck by lightning.

—Mark Twain

The trial was at hand. All the great lords and barons of Brandenburgh were assembled in the Hall of Justice in the ducal palace.

—Mark Twain

It is easy to show that the wish-fulfillment in dreams is often undisguised and easy to recognize, so that one may wonder why the language of dreams has not long since been understood.

—Sigmund Freud

On the occasion of this domestic little party, I did not repeat my former extensive preparations. I merely provided a pair of soles, a small leg of mutton, and a pigeon pie.

—Charles Dickens

Use a dash before such expressions as *namely, for example, that is,* and *for instance* which introduce an appositional element. If the appositional element is internal, of course use dashes on both sides of it:

Some California universities put a strong emphasis on athletics—for example, the University of Southern California and the University of California at Los Angeles.

Cultured people in England, in one matter at least, are more accurate than Americans—namely, the observance of the distinction between *can* and *may* and a similar one between *shall* and *will.*

There are power projects in nearly all the Far Western states—that is, Washington, California, Oregon, Idaho, Montana, Wyoming, Nevada, Arizona, Colorado, and New Mexico.

Use a dash before a summarizing expression:

The psychopathology of everyday life, the
interpretation of dreams, wit and its relation to
the unconscious, the theory of sex—all are
themes which Sigmund Freud dealt with in his
Basic Writings.
The history of the Hawaiian islands, its peoples,
flora and fauna—all are covered by James A.
Michener in his well-known book *Hawaii*.

A dash is used to indicate an unfinished or interrupted statement:

"But Michael—"
"My name's Heather. About that job as
secretary—"
"Aha!" Mr. Palis stepped back. "Won't you"—he
seemed to have difficulty getting his words out—
"come in?"
"Please stop—" he stuttered and stammered,
"that noise is driving me crazy!"

If a sentence concludes with a dash, no period is used or needed:

"The opportunity to tutor, the chance for both
intellectual and artistic achievement, the as-
sociation with a great learning institution—"
She broke off and concluded, "I know you will
find me qualified for the position."

Use the dash to set off appositional material if it:

(a) contains internal punctuation
(b) is in the nature of a repetition, an
afterthought, a correction, or an expla-
nation

(c) is strongly parenthetical
(d) is strongly contrasted or is antithetical
(e) is in the nature of a list of items

He was anti everything—stock market regulation, social security, trade unions—and just about every other type of economic control.

The main thesis of my book is supported by my research—supported, I maintain, beyond any reasonable doubt.

Andy Rooney—breezy, penetrating, irreverent, witty—epitomizes TV journalism in the 1980's.

I wonder—oh how I wonder—how he could have perpetuated this inane drivel and call it writing?

Security—not frivolous expenditure—is our sole concern.

We may—or may not—choose to join the country club at this time.

The American historians—Beard, Turner, Commons, Ross—gave him his first insight into the history of the United States.

Usually the dash can replace the colon. The dash is more emphatic, less formal, and less subtle than the colon:

We have sales representatives in most of the major cities: New York, Los Angeles, Chicago, San Francisco, Boston, Philadelphia, etc.

OR

We have sales representatives in most of the major cities—New York, Los Angeles, Chicago, San Francisco, Boston, Philadelphia, etc.

Sherman said: "War is hell."

OR

Sherman said—"War is hell."

Campers will need several things: a tent, flashlight, blankets, and hiking boots.

OR

Campers will need several things—a tent, flashlight, blankets, and hiking boots.

ELLIPSES

Ellipses: From Latin *ellipsis;* from
Greek, *ellipses,* a falling
short; from *ellipsein,* to
leave in or behind, to
leave out.

Ellipses points (. . .) are used to indicate the omission of a word or words necessary to the complete grammatical construction of a sentence. Sometimes this omission is intentional and sometimes it is not.

At once capturing the meaning and usage of ellipses, Don Marquis once wrote about ellipses in this fashion:

> When you see . . . three little dots . . . such as these . . . in the stuff of a modern versifier . . . even in our stuff . . . it means that the writer is trying to suggest something rather . . . well, elusive, if you get what we mean . . . and the reason he suggests it instead of expressing it . . . is . . . very often . . . because it is an almost idea . . . instead of a real idea.

Any omission from a quoted passage, whether it be a word, phrase, line, or paragraph, must be marked by the use of three dots . . . or ellipses. (NOTE: Do not use asterisks!)

Charles Dickins' book *David Copperfield* begins: "Whether I shall turn out to be the hero of my own life, or whether that station will be held by

65

anybody else, these pages must show. To begin
my life with the beginning of my life . . ."

Three dots indicate an omission within a sentence:

"In consideration of the day and hour of my
birth, it was declared . . . that I was destined to
be unlucky in life."

Ellipses are used to show an intentional omission from a sentence or quotation:

"The little girls wore elaborate hairdos. Some
wore their hair in pigtails, others had exaggerated
Afros, and still others an intricate arrangement
of braids worn like a crown."
    With ellipses:
"The little girls wore elaborate hairdos. Some . . .
pigtails, others . . . Afros, and still others . . .
intricate braids."

Ellipses can indicate that a listing or enumeration continues beyond the items named:

At two, she could recite the alphabet beautifully:
A, B, C . . .
Eggs, milk, flour . . . you will need all these
ingredients and more!
I love all my English classes, grammar,
punctuation, precis writing . . .
(In this case ellipses take the place and have the
meaning of "and so forth" or etc.")

Ellipses may be used to leave a sentence unfinished or to indicate an abrupt change of thought:

"Why didn't you . . ."
"You're leaving me!" the proprietor stormed.
"After I've spent all this time and money
training . . ."

"My mother doesn't understand . . ." "When I know all these things, I'm going to write a book . . ." "But how can they believe . . ."

A question mark or exclamation point may follow ellipses points (three only):

Who will attend? Sam? Carol? Alice . . .?
I hate it! I hate it! It's loathsome . . .!
You are leaving me . . .!
I don't understand . . .!
But how can that be . . .?

Ellipses may be used to indicate faltering speech:

I don't know . . . I just can't . . . well, my thoughts are . . . you see . . . so don't blame me . . . if . . .

Ellipses are often used to show a missing line from a poem:

I knew your eyes by heart
. . .
I could repeat them in detail,
remembering their elements in pearls
   and moonstones
in the dark wing of a starling . . .
and the bright morning faces of asters.

When ellipses end a sentence, a fourth dot, representing the period must be used:

She had many acquaintances among writers and artists, but psychologists and psychiatrists were her special interest. . . .

Suppose I start to walk down that path and down that road and . . . .

She was a thin, sparse-haired widow of 26 wearing a blue smock, blue trousers, and a conical bamboo hat. . . .

THE VIRGULE

> **Virgule:** From Latin, *virgula,* "little rod."

The virgule, or slash mark, is a slanting line (/) used to mark the division of words or lines.

The virgule is used in the expression *and/or* :

You will find lots of data and/or reference points meaning a choice between three alternate choices.

Boys and/or girls may mean boys, just girls, or boys and girls . . .

You can write dates in an informal manner by using a virgule:

FORMAL: June 19, 1988
INFORMAL: 6/19/87

The virgule is sometimes used in place of the word *as*:

600/500   (In this case, 600 units are to be shipped and only 500 units billed.)

The virgule is used to separate lines of poetry when the poetry is quoted in prose style:

Autumn is here/And with it comes the plover's cry/The plover who
has lost his mate/on Sao River's misty banks.

The virgule replaces *and* in some compounds:

Sales have slumped in the August/September period.

The expression "in care of" is frequently abbreviated as:

C/O

The virgule is used to represent the word *per* :

The car was traveling 60 miles/hour.
The workers were on strike for a wage of
$15/hour.
The hotel room costs $100/day.

BRACKETS

Brackets: From French, diminutive
of *brague*, breeches;
From Latin, *braca*, akin
to breeches.

Brackets are used to enclose corrections, additions, comments, and quoted material. You will find brackets on newer typewriter keyboards as well as computer keyboards, but if you are working with an older model typewriter, it may be necessary to hand draw them. Of course, typesetting equipment is capable of producing brackets, and the typesetter, following your instructions, will add them where necessary.

Brackets should never be confused with parentheses which have an entirely different use. Parentheses are used to enclose *your own* parenthetical statements. Brackets are used to insert matter into *someone else's* writing which you are quoting or editing.

Brackets are used to set off an editor's comments from a printed text:

This portrait of [Theodore Roosevelt] is
exceptional.
This signature is an authentic one belonging to
[Benjamin] Franklin.
He said, "I am very annoyed." [annoyed? He was
insane with fury!]. . . .

71

They were staying with the author [i.e., Louisa
May Alcott] in Massachusetts.

"The jury awarded $5,000 [$10,000] to the
plaintiff."

"Let them [all the sons who have abandoned the
paternal house] return."

**You may use brackets to insert material within something
already in parentheses:**

(Newton [Mass.], April 1970)

(Many corrections were made in the fourth
[1981] edition.)

(It was signed on the third [fourth] of July.)

(She was born in Santa Monica, [Calif.] in the
spring.)

**To call attention to an error in quoted material, you may
use the Latin word *sic* (meaning *thus it is*) and enclose it in
brackets to indicate the error is in the original material and
is not that of the editor:**

"All the merchandise in the shops are [*sic*]
discounted," he announced.

"I acted with wilful [*sic*] disregard of the law."

Ynyok Tsin [*sic*] had to keep her diseased
husband away from public view.

(In the latter example, *sic* indicates that the
spelling of the name, though unusual, is correct.)

**Brackets may be used to fill in where words have been
omitted from a quotation:**

The advertisement read: "These pants [denim,
twill, wool] were shipped here from Ireland."

"In the third act of the opera, she [Aida] is
betrayed."

"They [the British] were just as much at fault as their enemy [the Germans]," said the professor.

Brackets can also be used in printing stage directions for some plays:

[Burton exits.]

You may use brackets to indicate the phonetic spelling of a word:

allot [a-lŏt']

THE AMPERSAND

Ampersand: Alteration of *and per se and*

The sign & is used to represent the word *and*. This character usually was included at the end of the alphabet in such early children's books as the *Hornbook,* an early primer, which consisted of a single page protected by a sheet of horn, used to teach children to read. The word is thought to represent a contraction of *and per se and.* The children used to repeat the alphabet out loud and describe the ampersand as *A per se A*, from which its present name is derived.

The origin of this mark is lost in the mists of time. Some scholars believe the mark was created by early scribes in order to minimize the number of letters they had to write. It is also thought to be an abbreviation of the Latin *et* meaning and. Others think that perhaps early printers invented the mark to squeeze in the word *and* at the end of a line where space was scarce. Today, the ampersand is chiefly used by business firms such as Panise & Son, Gilson & Daughters, Strumpf & Associates, and Chuzzlewit & Bros.

QUOTATION MARKS

> ***Quote:*** Medieval Latin from Latin, feminine of *quotus*, "of what number."

Quotation marks, both double ("...") and single ('...') are marks of enclosure for words, clauses or phrases, sentences, paragraphs, and even multiple paragraphs which by definition indicate what someone has said or written.

Use quotation marks to enclose a direct quotation:

"His idea of a seven course dinner is a taco and a six-pack," she said in exasperation.

Do not use quotation marks to enclose an indirect quotation:

She told me her boyfriend's idea of a seven course dinner was a taco and a six-pack.

Begin a direct quotation with a capital letter:

My teacher said, "Complete the assignment in study hall."
She told the boss, "I quit! I hate this job!"
He said, "The movie starts at eight o'clock. We will have to hurry."
My professor opined, "English is unmistakably one language, with two major national dialects: British and American."

When the quoted matter is a sentence fragment, it does not begin with a capital:

> The movie critic said the film was "in the great tradition."
> The book reviewer called the new best-seller a "monumental waste of paper, ink, and time."

When quoted matter is divided in two parts by such expressions as *he said, she replied, John added,* etc., the second part begins with a small letter:

> "Go home and get to bed," he said, "before you come down with a cold."
> "Watch out!" Polly yelled, "the kitchen floor has just been waxed."

Of course, if the second part of a broken quotation is a new sentence, it begins with a capital letter:

> "Drive carefully," he instructed. "The roads are slick with snow and ice."
> "I think you'll enjoy this new ethnic restaurant," he told me. "Hermione and I eat there all the time."

A direct quotation is set off from the rest of the sentence by commas:

> Anthony told me, "A very still and blank interval ensued, and then I felt the hand of a policeman on my shoulder."
> I remember his exact words, "Well, I must say— but look here, let me walk the floor a little, my mind is getting into a sort of whirl."
> At West Point the bugle is supposed to be saying, "I can't get 'em up, I can't get 'em up, I can't get 'em up in the morning!"

Use quotation marks to enclose a word or phrase that defines:

The word "toro" is Spanish for bull.
In this context, the term "Minority Small Business" is used to mean one with fewer than 100 employees.

To quote an entire paragraph that is a direct quotation, place quotation marks at the beginning of the paragraph and at the end:

"Yes, by George, you did say 'shall'! You are the most definite devil I ever saw in the matter of language. Dear, dear, dear, look here! Definite speech means clarity of mind. Upon my word I believe you've got what you believe to be a rational reason for venturing into this house, an entire stranger, on this wild scheme of buying the wool crop of an entire colony on speculation. Bring it out—I am prepared—acclimatized, if I may use the word. Why would you buy the crop and why would you make that sum out of it? That is to say, what makes you think you—"

—Mark Twain, *Cecil Rhodes and the Shark*

Quoted Material That Extends Over More Than One Paragraph

Use a quotation mark at the beginning of *each paragraph* but not at the end when the same person is talking. Use a quotation mark at the end of the last and final paragraph only:

> "I was going on at a great rate, with a clenched hand, and a most enthusiastic countenance; but it was quite unnecessary to proceed.
>
> "I had said enough. I had done it again. Oh, she was so frightened!
>
> "I thought I had killed her, this time. I sprinkled water on her face. I went down on my knees. I plucked at my hair. I denounced myself as a remorseless brute and a ruthless beast. I implored her forgiveness."
>
> —Charles Dickens,
> *David Copperfield*

Quotation Marks With Other Marks of Punctuation

Commas and periods are *always* placed inside the closing quotation marks.

There are no exceptions to this rule in American usage. And it is one of the rules of punctuation that is frequently misused:

> "I know," he told me happily, "that we can finish the job today."

"You look beautiful," he smiled, "that color
suits you to a T."
"Thomas," my grandfather admonished, "it's
time you got up and went to work."

NOTE: For those who went to school in Great
Britain or who read a lot of British texts and/or
literature, it should be noted that this rule is just
the opposite in those countries.

**Semicolons and colons are placed inside the closed
quotation when they are a part of the quotation; otherwise
they are placed outside:**

Today my teacher said, "I'd like you to read the
following authors by the end of the semester:
Shakespeare, Homer, Proust, and Milton."
My teacher described as "highbrow reading":
Shakespeare, Homer, Proust, the Bible, and
Milton.

**Question marks and exclamation marks are placed inside
the closed quotation when they are a part of the quotation,
otherwise they are placed outside:**

"How difficult you can be!" she cried.
"Are the players ready?" asked the umpire.
My heart fell when I heard the official exclaim,
"Your plane has left!"
Were you surprised when he said, "I'll be glad to
come to your party"?

**Thoughts—when they are the exact words in which the
character thinks them—may be placed in quotation marks:**

He thought, "Surely I will go mad if I don't get
out of this disorganized, messy, disruptive office.

79

I cannot think of a worse environment for a
creative worker."
Her thoughts seemed to chase each other round
and round like horses racing around the course at
Santa Anita. "How did I get in this pickle and
how will I get out? Every choice I seem to have
appears to lead directly to disaster. Every option I
have is fraught with dire misfortune."

Use single quotation marks to enclose a quotation within a quotation:

I remember her instructions clearly, "For
tomorrow read Robert Frost's poem, 'Mending
Wall.' "
Napoleon often bragged, "The word 'impossible'
is not in my dictionary."
"The BBC's 'This Week in Westminster' is my
favorite radio program," confessed Sallie.

Use quotation marks to indicate a misnomer or special meaning for a word:

Be careful of so-called "antiques"; many might
more properly be called junk.
What she called "luxuries," I called
indispensable comforts.
A "brass hat" is an officer at least one rank
higher than your own.
She said they were "faux" diamonds, not
knowing that the word was merely French for
false.
She liked to say she was an "amanuensis"
which amused everyone but the other
secretaries.

(NOTE: Don't overdo this usage. It can become
cloying and offensive when it is overly used.)

Use quotation marks to enclose titles of television programs, articles, songs, short stories, essays, poems, and the like:

> He prefers to spend his evenings at home watching "Star Trek" reruns.
> His favorite song is Elvis Presley's "Hound Dog."
> I thoroughly enjoyed reading Doris Lessing's short story "A Man and Two Women."
> Read Chapter 12, "The Victorian Poets."

With dialogue—two or more persons having a conversation—begin a new paragraph each time the speaker changes:

> "My own! May I mention something?"
> "Oh, please don't be practical!" said Dora coaxingly. "Because it frightens me so!"
> "Sweetheart!" I returned; "there is nothing to alarm you in all of this. I want you to think of it quite differently. I want to make it nerve you, and inspire you, Dora!"
> "Oh, but that's so shocking!" cried Dora.
> "My love, no. Perseverance and strength of character will enable us to bear much worse things."
> "But I haven't got any strength at all," said Dora, shaking her curls. "Have I, Jip? Oh, do kiss, Jip, and be agreeable!"

CAPITALIZATION

> ***Capital:*** From Latin, *capitalis*, "of the head."

Capitalize the first word of every sentence. That's a rule with which everyone is familiar. But other rules of capitalization are sometimes not so clear. Since capitalization is closely allied with punctuation in making the meaning of your sentences crystal clear, we are devoting a chapter to its discussion.

The first word of every sentence is capitalized:

This architectural curiosity, Hearst Castle, was designed to house William Randolph Hearst's vast art collection. Each of the three-and-one-half hour tours offers a different look at the mammoth *La Casa Grande*.

Capitalize the names of the days of the week and the months:

Sunday	January	July
Monday	February	August
Tuesday	March	September
Wednesday	April	October
Thursday	May	November
Friday	June	December
Saturday		

Do not capitalize the seasons:

spring
summer
autumn
winter

NOTE: The only time these words are capitalized is when they are personified. This occurs mainly in poetry:

"Winter, in her dress of white . . ."
"O Spring, you goddess, all decked in finery's green . . ."

Capitalize the first and all important words in the names of publications, works of art, etc. However, do not capitalize *the* unless it is a specific part of the title:

the Los Angeles Times
the Saturday Evening Post
The Grapes of Wrath
The Journal of Religion
Gainsborough's "Blue Boy"
Van Gogh's "Starry Night"

Normally, you do not capitalize prepositions, conjunctions, or articles:

Gone with the Wind
The Proud and the Damned
The Bold and the Beautiful

Trade names are capitalized:

Bon Ami	Dom Perignon
Xerox	Sweet Corporal
Pyrex	Gucci
Plexiglass	Jaguar
Rye-crisp	Rolls Royce
Coca Cola (But a cola drink)	

The names of specific streets, buildings, and parks are capitalized:

Fifth Avenue
The Empire State Building
The Flatiron Building
Park Avenue
Route #66
Sunset Boulevard

Of course, when used generically, such terms as *park, street, building, boulevard, route, avenue,* etc., are not capitalized:

> She lives in a busy boulevard.
> Her house overlooks a pretty park.
> Do you live on this street?
> Let's drive down the route by the ocean.

Titles are capitalized when they *precede* a name:

President Ronald Reagan
Governor Mario Cuomo
Senator Ted Kennedy
Representative Joe Wachs
Mayor Tom Bradley

When used *without a name,* these titles are not capitalized, one only exception being *President* when it refers to the President of the United States:

> George Deukmejian, who is the present governor of California
> Mario Cuomo, the governor of the state of New York
> Barry Goldwater, the former senator from Arizona
> EXCEPTION: Ronald Reagan, who is the President of the United States . . .

Military titles are capitalized when used in direct address, otherwise they are written lower case:

DIRECT	INDIRECT
General Ulysses S. Grant	the general
Admiral Chester W. Nimitz	the admiral
Sergeant John Doe	the sergeant
Private John Doe	the private

Religious titles and offices are capitalized when used in direct address, otherwise they are written lower case:

DIRECT	INDIRECT
Pope John XXIII	the pope; papacy
Cardinal Francis Spellman	the cardinal
Archbishop Makarios III	the archbishop
Rabbi Stephen Wise	the rabbi
the Reverend James Neal, Minister of All Saints	the minister
Mother Superior Mary Margaret	the mother superior of the convent

Lower case family names when not followed by a given name:

Uncle Tom   my uncle and aunt
Sister Sally   my sister and brothers
my Nephew John   my niece and baby nephew

Capitalize all geographical locations:

The Seine River	Lake Michigan
The Sahara Desert	The Gulf of Mexico
New York City	The Eternal City
The South Pole	The Dominion of
Rome, Italy	Canada
the Orient	the Occident
Europe	the Americas
Paris, France	

Government agencies and departments are usually capitalized:

the House of Representatives	the United Nation
the Senate	the Russian Embassy
the Department of Labor	the Connecticut
the General Assembly of California	State Highway Commission
the Ways and Means Committee	

Capitalize most holidays and festivals:

Christmas	D-Day
Easter	V-J Day
Thanksgiving	Boxing Day
Passover	Shrove Tuesday
Yom Kippur	Valentine's Day
the Fourth of July	Memorial Day

Capitalize names and proper nouns as well as derivatives of proper nouns:

Robin N. Rap   Asian
Lucille Darrell   English
Don M. Muchmore   Elizabethan
Clark Gable   Norwegian
Walter Cronkite   Shakespearean

Names of study courses are not capitalized unless they refer to a specific course:

"He plans to study chemistry, physics, and biology and has already signed up for Biology I."
"I am looking forward to my Physics II class this fall."
"Her school curriculum includes journalism, typing, and English III.

Political organizations, movements, and affiliations are always capitalized:

He always votes the Democratic ticket.
He's a member of the Republican club.
They called themselves Bolsheviks.
the Conservative Party
the Labour Party
the Communist party

NOTE: "Party" following the name of a political organization may be capitalized or not, according to the dictates of your editor. Either way is correct.

Religion, religious groups, the names of the deity and personal pronouns standing for the deity, including the devil ("Satan"), are all capitalized:

Baptist	Moslem	The Ten
Catholic	Buddha	Commandments
Episcopalian	Bible	the Apocrypha
God	Scriptures	the Blessed Virgin
Satan	the Talmud	the Koran
the Book of Job	Lord's Prayer	the Book of Genesis

Capitalize abbreviations which stand for words which are capitalized:

M.D.	D.E.A.
Ph.D.	D.D.S.

Do not capitalize the following:

a.m.

p.m.

ITALICS

Italics: From Latin *Italicus*, of
ancient Italy.

Italics, a style of printing in which the characters
slant to the right, first appeared in an Italian
version of Virgil, the *Aldine Virgil*, printed in
Venice in 1501.

The signal used to tell a printer to italicize certain
words, sentences, or large blocks of copy is
<u>underlining</u>.

Set the Following in Italics

1. Titles of books and magazines:

Red Storm Rising
More Die of Heartbreak
Empire
Saturday Review
The Atlantic Monthly

2. Names of ships, trains, and aircraft:

The QE II (ship)
The Super Chief (train)
The Concorde (aircraft)

3. Titles of motion pictures, plays, operas, and epic poems:

Beverly Hills Cop (movie)
Death of a Salesman (play)
Aïda (opera)
Aeneid (epic poem)

4. Names of newspapers:

The Times of London
The New York Times
The Los Angeles Herald Examiner

NOTE: Only the actual name of the newspaper should be underlined. If "the" is not part of the formal title, it should not be underlined, nor should the word "newspaper" or "magazine" be underlined unless it is part of the name: The Los Angeles *Times* newspaper, The Boston *Herald*, etc.

5. Names of legal cases:

Marbury vs. Madison
Brown v. the Board of Education

6. Foreign words of phrases:

Caveat Emptor! (Latin, let the buyer beware)
Zeitgeist (German, spirit of the time)
Merci beaucoup (French, thank you very much)
La tour d'ivoire (French, The ivory tower)

7. Latin (scientific) names of genus and species:

Musca domestica (house fly)
Felix Libyea domestica (cat)
Mus musculus (mouse)
Siphonaptera (flea)

Additional Rules Regarding Italics

8. Italicize a word, figure, or letter whenever it is used nearly as a name and not to represent an idea:

Words which end in *-able* or *-ible* always create spelling problems for me.

Do you prefer *theatre* or *theater?*
Don't forget to dot your *i*'s and cross your *t*'s and watch your *p*'s and *q*'s!

9. Designate italics for letters used to represent persons in the following type of sentence:

A will receive one-third of the estate, *B* will get one-tenth, and *C* receives the entire remainder.

10. Stage directions are italized and usually placed in brackets:

LARRY: [*Wringing his hands impatiently.*] I cannot wait another minute!

LOIS: [*Coyly.*] I should think you'd want to see how it all comes out!

LARRY: [*With a tinge of resignation.*] Oh, all right. All right. But this business can go on all night!

LOIS: [*Placating.*] Not at all. It will soon be over. And think what a thrill it will be to know . . . to finally know.

11. Italicize any word, sentence, or paragraph for emphasis:

Sam was told to move by the first of the month *or else.*
A wise man knows when *not* to talk.
The wines were *very* different.
Every 3,000 miles, change the oil and filter—*that's* how a responsible car owner behaves.

NUMBERS

Confusion runs rampant over the proper use of numbers—figures or words? Here are some simple rules which will help to dispel confusion.

Write numbers from one to ten in *words:*

She is one of the most beautiful women I have ever seen. In fact, I would rate her as a "ten" on a scale of one to ten—ten being best.

Write numbers from 11 up in figures:

There are 11 secretaries in our office all of whom weigh over 200 lbs. A diet doctor could make a fortune in our department.

Do not start a sentence with a number in figures. Always write it in words:

"Fifteen men on the dead man's chest"—Robert Louis Stevenson
"Thirty acres and a mule."—Erskine Caldwell

Spell out round numbers above one hundred.

He paid hundreds of thousands of dollars for that original painting.
I think that ninety-nine persons out of a hundred would give the same answer.

Spell out fractions when they stand alone in texts:

I believe that nine-tenths of his success is a result of his charming manner.

The bill only needs a two-thirds majority to pass, not a three-fourths majority as was originally thought.

He was mad because he spent three-quarters of an hour to buy a quarter of a pound of butter at the grocery store.

To avoid confusion, write out a number which precedes a fraction, and write the fractions in figures:

He bought two ¾ stakes.
seven ⅞-inch pieces
ten ¹¹/₃₂-inch bites

Spell out numbers referring to centuries, military bodies, political divisions, and sessions of congress:

the twentieth century	the Twenty-Fourth
the Fifth Cavalry	Division
	the Seventy-sixth
	Congress

When writing dates, use figures except when the number precedes the name of the month, in which case you may use figures or write it in words:

August 20, 1987
September 22, 1924
The meeting will take place on the seventeenth of April, 1988.
The convention is set for the eighth of October, 1989.

Spell out the age of a person.

My daughter is sixteen years of age.
She claims to be twenty-eight, but I would say she is closer to thirty-five.

They have two children—a girl, aged six, and a boy, aged two.

Use figures for pages, chapters, sections, etc.:

page 78   chapters 9–15
chapter 6   Gate 8
book 3   Please see time table 17.

Write out numerals as compound modifiers:

a twenty-two inch waist
a ten-gallon hat
a twenty-seven inch pipe
a three-by-five card

Spell out sums of money if the amount:

    (a) is less than one dollar;
    (b) occurs in isolated instances;
    (c) serves as a modifier

I had thirty-seven cents in my coin purse.
His wallet contained two twenty-dollar bills, four five-dollar bills, and some coins.
She said her new dress cost her seventy-eight dollars.

Percentages are written in figures as are mathematical figures:

His mortgage rate was 10 percent.
Her Certificate of Deposit was earning 9.2 per cent interest.
Multiply by 2 to find the correct answer.
He bought three 8½ per cent bonds.

DIACRITICAL MARKS

Diacritic: Adjective from Greek, *diakritikos*, to distinguish.

The principal diacritical of accent marks include acute, cedilla, circumflex, dieresis, grave, tilde, and umlaut. Encountered primarily in foreign languages—particularly French—accent marks tend to be eliminated once the foreign word is assimilated into the English language. Even so, a passing acquaintance with accent marks is important. Sometimes a word will appear in one publication with an accent mark and without it in another. A foreign word tends to retain its accent marks when it first begins to be used, and then they are gradually dropped.

Here are some words which originally used an accent mark to indicate that the accented vowel is pronounced as a long *a*, a fact made clear by the use of the acute accent with which the word was originally spelled in English and still is in French:

attaché	éclat
blasé	fiancé
cliché	naiveté
communiqué	passé
coupé	précis
début	résumé
éclair	touché

Cedilla

It is placed under the letter *c* in many words which are borrowed from foreign languages to indicate that it is pronounced as a soft *s* instead of as a *k*, which is the more usual. In most cases, the cedilla has been dropped from words such as facade and soupcon since these words have been assimilated into the English language.

Here are some other words which retain the cedilla in the French language:

> Français garçon aperçu Provençal

Circumflex

The circumflex is used over certain vowels in some languages (notably French) to indicate a specific sound or quality of the vowel:

bête noire	tête à tête
crêpe de Chine	coupe de grâce
papier mâché	pâté de foie gras
raison d'être	table d'hôte

In English, for all of the above, you are most apt to encounter the circumflex in the word *tête à tête* as many publications print this phrase (head-to-head) with the original circumflex.

Diaeresis

This is a mark consisting of two dots used to indicate separation of two consecutive vowels into separate syllables. It is used, for example, to show that the first two syllables of zoölogy and coöperation are pronounced separately. You may wish to use the diaeresis with such words as reëxamine, reënlist, or naïve, although the first two are most commonly written re-examine and reenlist. American publications have long since dropped the diaeresis from naive.

Grave Accent

This mark tells you to pronounce the letter *e* as in the word "bear," and the letter *a* as in "ah." Poets often use this accent mark to indicate that the syllables normally run together, or elided, are to be pronounced separately—movèd (mov-ed) or lovèd (lov-ed). Here are some words which originally used a grave accent. Some publications still retain them.

crème   frère
pied-à-terre   suède
père

Tilde

A tilde tells the reader to pronounce the *n* as *ny*. The tilde is most familiarly used in the Spanish language, but it is also used quite frequently in the Portuguese language. Here are some examples:

cañon	(spelled canyon in English)
doña	(don-ya)
mañana	(man-yana)
señor	(sen-yor)

Umlaut

The umlaut is a diacritical mark consisting of two dots indicating a vowel partially assimilated by the next sound. It is characteristic of the German language and is sometimes used by careful writers. You will probably encounter the umlaut in proper names such as Dürer, Tannhäuser, Brüning, and Göring.

Two brand names which retain diacritical marks even in their American advertisements are Moët & Chandon and Kahlúa. In the first instance, the diaeresis indicates that the two vowels are pronounced separately and in the latter, that the accent is on the *u*. French words that you are apt to see in print retaining diacritical marks include:

à la carte	habitué	paté
à la mode	ingénue	pièce de résistence
attaché	lycée	protegé
consommé	mère	roué
coup d'état	née	sauté
éclat	outré	piñata
exposé	fête	vis-à-vis
frappé		

GLOSSARY

ACRONYM:—An acronym is a word formed from the initial letters of a name such as Women's Army Corp to form WAC or radio detecting and ranging to form RADAR.

AMPERSAND:—An ampersand is a mark or sign (&) used to represent the word *and*.

APPOSITIVE/APPOSITION:—An appositive is a word or phrase which follows a noun or pronoun and explains that noun or pronoun. A word or phrase said to be in *apposition* has the same meaning.

Example:

One important trait, determination, he had in abundance.
Here, the word *determination* is in apposition to *trait*. It helps to define *trait* and must be set off by commas.

Example:

Mary, wearing a red ribbon in her hair, is my classmate.
Wearing a red ribbon in her hair helps to define *Mary*. It is a phrase in apposition to the word "Mary."

ARTICLES:—*A, an, the. A* and *an* are called indefinite articles (*a pencil, an apple*). *The* is a definite article (*the lawyer, the teacher, the book*).

CLAUSE:—When a noun and verb are joined together (married, in a sense) they form a clause. *The clouds gathered.* This clause makes sense. It is complete. It is called an independent clause. When two of these clauses are joined end to end, *The clouds gathered. The storm approached*, a compound sentence is formed. To join the two clauses, either place a semicolon between them or use a comma, followed by coordinating conjunction (and, but, or, nor, for, yet, so).

Examples:

The clouds gathered; the storm approached.
The clouds gathered, and the storm approached.
The clouds gathered, for the storm approached.

COMMA FAULT:—The specific error of joining two complete sentences (two complete statements) with a comma instead of a semicolon is known as a comma fault.

COMMA FAULT: The clouds gathered, the storm approached.

CORRECT USAGE: The clouds gathered; the storm approached.

COMPLEX SENTENCE:—A sentence containing one independent clause and one or more dependent (subordinate) clauses is called a complex sentence.

100

Example:

If I don't complete the exam today, I can retake it in July.

COMPOUND SUBJECTS:—When two or more subjects join two or more predicates, the subjects are identified as compound subjects, while the predicates are identified as compound predicates.

Example:

The BMW and Jaguar twisted and turned on the track.

CONJUNCTION:—A conjunction is a linking or joining word. (You can remember this by linking *junction* to *joining*.) Commonly used conjunctions include *but, and, or, at, as, of,* and *by.*

CONTRACTION:—A contraction is a shortened form of a word, such as can't for cannot, didn't for did not, etc.

DEPENDENT CLAUSE:—If a clause cannot stand by itself and make sense, it is called a dependent or subordinate clause. It must be joined to an independent clause to make a complex sentence. The most common of the three types of dependent clauses is the adverb dependent clause that answers the question when? where? why? how? or how much? If an adverb dependent clause begins a complex sentence, it will always be followed by a comma:

When she shops, she always buys fresh produce.

But when the adverb dependent clause is at the end of the sentence, there is no comma separating it: She always buys fresh produce when she shops.

The other two types of dependent clauses are the noun and adjective dependent clauses. These are samples of noun dependent clauses:

That she is a fine woman really surprises me. (*That she is a fine woman* serves as the subject of the entire sentence.)

I really like what he did.

(*What he did* is a noun dependent clause serving as a direct object since it's receiving the action of the predicate *like*.) Two examples of adjective dependent clauses are:

The man, who is my uncle, is a sweet guy.

("*. . . is a sweet guy*" describes the man.)

He sat on the table, *which promptly broke*.

(*. . . which promptly broke* is an adjectival dependent clause describing table.)

DIACRITICAL MARKS:—A diacritical mark is an aid to pronunciation, used chiefly in foreign languages and in many foreign words and phrases which have crossed over into English.

DIRECT QUOTATION:—A direct quotation cites the actual words written by someone else.

ELLIPSES:—The omissions of a word or words is shown by the use of three dots called ellipses. Sometimes a dash may be used to denote omission.

Apostrophes are used to show omission in contractions.

END-STOP:—An end-stop is a term used to refer to any and all marks at the end of a sentence. A period is the most common end-stop. However, a question mark, exclamation mark, or ellipses, when ending a sentence, may serve as end-stops. End-stop is another term for *terminal mark*.

INDEFINITE PRONOUN:—Indefinite pronouns are less exact in meaning than pronouns. More frequently used indefinite pronouns include *another, any, anyone, anything, everybody, everyone, everything, few, many, nobody, none, no one, one, several, some, someone,* and *something.*

INDIRECT QUESTION:—An indirect question is often in the form of a request. Direct question: When can you leave work? Indirect question: She asked when I could leave work.

INTERROGATIVE SENTENCE:—An interrogative sentence asks a question and ends with a question mark.

LOWER CASE:—Lower case or small letters are distinguished from upper case or capital letters.

MODIFY:—To modify is to limit or change the meaning of a word:
a beautiful girl (*beautiful* modifies or limits *girl*)
an ugly girl (*ugly* changes the meaning of *girl*)

Adjectives modify nouns and pronouns. Adverbs modify verbs, adjectives, and other adverbs.

NONRESTRICTIVE CLAUSE OR PHRASE:— Nonrestrictive means that *without the clause or phrase* the same point would be made. Such clauses or phrases are always set off by commas:

Mary, who is wearing a blue dress today, is my sister.

Sam, standing by the bar holding a beer, works in my office.

NOUN:—A noun is the name of a person, place, thing, or idea. There are four types of nouns: common, proper, concrete, and abstract.

PARTICIPLE:—A participle is a word which has the function of both verb and adjective. Present participles always end in *-ing* (walking, talking). The past participle has various forms in the passive voice (walked, talked, sung, kicked).

Examples:

The ball *kicked* by the boys, went over the wall.
Singing loudly, he adjusted the knobs of the shower.

PERIOD FAULT:—A phrase or dependent clause cannot be written as a complete sentence. Using a period, terminal mark, or end-stop after such a phrase is called the period fault.

PHRASE:—A phrase is a group of related words which does not contain a subject or predicate. A phrase is used as a part of speech, the equivalent of a noun, adjective, or adverb.

PREFIX:—A prefix is a syllable or syllables added at the beginning of a word to change its meaning. Adding *pre* to *school* gives us *preschool*, adding *in* to *sane* creates *insane*.

PREPOSITION:—A preposition is a linking or joining word which shows the relationship of a noun or pronoun to some other word in the sentence. Prepositions show position or direction (at, with, to, from) or indicate cause or possession (because, of, from). (Use the *position* in pre*position* to remember that a preposition indicates position or direction.)

PRONOUN:—A pronoun's name describes its function. A pronoun is *pro* or *for* a noun. A pronoun is the "stand in" for the real thing. "She" for Alice, "He" for Tom; "Everyone" for the group; "Hers" for what belongs to Rita, and so on. Common pronouns include *I, me, mine, you, yours, he, him, his, she, her, hers, it, its, we, us, ours, they, them, theirs, myself, yourself, yourselves, himself, herself, ourselves, themselves, each one, everyone, anything, somebody,* etc.

RESTRICTIVE CLAUSES:—A restrictive clause or phrase is one which is necessary to the sentence.

Without it, the meaning of the sentence would change.

SUFFIX:—A syllable or syllables added at the end of a word to change its meaning is referred to as a suffix. Adding *ness* to *polite* gives us *politeness*, adding it to *kind* results in *kindness*.

VERB:—A verb refers to any word which describes action, occurrence, or being.

VIRGULE:—A diagonal mark (/) used especially to separate alternatives is called a virgule.

BIBLIOGRAPHY

A Manual of Style. 12th ed., revised, Chicago and London: The University of Chicago Press, 1969.

Clairborne, Robert. *The Birth of Writing.* New York: Time-Life Books, 1974.

Curme, George O. *English Grammar.* New York: The Barnes & Noble Outline Series, 1982.

Encyclopedia of English. Edited by Arthur Zeiger. New York: Arco Publishing Company, 1961.

Grammar Handbook. Oxford, England: Oxford University Press, 1985.

Howard, Philip. *The State of the Language: English Observed.* New York: Oxford University Press, 1985.

Pence, Raymond W. *Style Book in English.* New York: The Odyssey Press, 1964.

Pyles, Thomas and John Algeo. *The Origins and Development of the English Language.* 3rd ed. New York: Harcourt Brace Jovanovich, Inc., 1982.

Shaw, Harry. *Punctuate It Right!* New York: Barnes & Noble Books, 1983.

Strumpf, Michael and Auriel Douglas. *Painless Perfect Grammar*. New York: Monarch Press, 1985.

Venolia, Jan. *Write Right!* New York: Periwinkle Press, 1979.

Warriner, John E. and Francis Griffith. *English Grammar and Composition*. New York: Harcourt, Brace & World, 1963.

Words Into Type. 3rd ed. Englewood Cliffs, New Jersey: Prentice-Hall, Inc., 1974.

ROMAN NUMERALS

I.	1	LXX.	70
II.	2	LXXV.	75
III.	3	LXXIX.	79
IV.	4	LXXX.	80
V.	5	LXXXV.	85
VI.	6	LXXXIX.	89
VII.	7	XC.	90
VIII.	8	XCV.	95
IX.	9	XCIX.	99
X.	10	C.	100
XV.	15	CL.	150
XIX.	19	CC.	200
XX.	20	CCC.	300
XXV.	25	CD.	400
XXIX.	29	D.	500
XXX.	30	DC.	600
XXXV.	35	DCC.	700
XXXIX.	39	DCCC.	800
XL.	40	CM.	900
XLV.	45	M.	1,000
XLIX.	49	MD.	1,500
L.	50	MM.	2,000
LV.	55	MMM.	3,000
LIX.	59	MMMM or M$\overline{\text{V}}$	4,000
LX.	60	$\overline{\text{V}}$	5,000
LXV.	65	$\overline{\text{M}}$	1,000,000
LXIX.	69		

Dates

MDC.	1600	MCMXL.	1940
MDCC.	1700	MCML.	1950
MDCCC.	1800	MCMLX.	1960
MCM or MDCCCC.	1900	MCMLXX.	1970
MCMX.	1910	MCMLXXX.	1980
MCMXX.	1920	MCMXC.	1990
MCMXXX.	1930	MM.	2000

PROOFREADERS' MARKS

℉ Delete

⌒ Close up; delete space

℉ Delete and close up

Insert space

eq# Make space between words equal; make leading between lines equal

hr# Insert hair space

ls Letterspace

¶ Begin new paragraph

no ¶ Run paragraphs together

▢ Move type one em from left or right

lc Lowercase capital letter

cap Capitalize lowercase letter

sc Set in small capitals

ital Set in italic type

rom Set in roman type

bf Set in boldface type

wf Wrong font; set in correct type

× Reset broken letter; check repro or film

⌐ Reverse (type upside down)

⌐⌐ Move right	PUNCTUATION MARKS
⊏ Move left	⌒ Insert comma
⊐⊏ Center	ⱽ Insert apostrophe (or single quotation mark)
⌒ Move up	
⊔ Move down	ⱽⱽ Insert quotation marks
⸗ Straighten type; align horizontally	⊙ Insert period
‖ Align vertically	⦿? Insert question mark
tr Transpose	;∣ Insert semicolon
sp Spell out	:∣ Insert colon
stet Let it stand	∣=∣ Insert hyphen
↓ Push down type; check type image	ⱶ Insert em dash
	ⱶ Insert en dash

112

INDEX

115